Salmon Run: An Epic Journey to the Ocean and Back Again
Text and illustrations copyright © 2025 Annie Chen

Published in 2025 by Red Comet Press, LLC, Brooklyn, NY

All rights reserved. No part of this book may be used or reproduced in any manner whatsoever without written permission except in the case of brief quotations embodied in critical articles and reviews.

Library of Congress Control Number: 2024948536

ISBN (HB): 978-1-63655-165-4
ISBN (EBOOK): 978-1-63655-166-1

25 26 27 28 29 TLF 10 9 8 7 6 5 4 3 2 1

First Edition
Manufactured in China
Red Comet Press is distributed by ABRAMS, New York

RedCometPress.com

SALMON RUN

AN EPIC *journey* TO THE *ocean* AND *back*

ANNIE *chen*

RED *comet* PRESS • *brooklyn*

On a crisp autumn day, a Pacific salmon is born.

She begins her life in the cool waters of the Duwamish River, surrounded by the lush green forest of the Pacific Northwest.

days 2-45

She is a tiny orange egg, smaller than a pea! Soft and delicate, she is surrounded by hundreds of eggs in a nest of rocks, called a redd.

This redd shields her from swift currents and dangerous predators.

days 2–45

Inside each egg is an embryo, which is what a baby is called before it hatches, and a bright orange yolk. The yolk, a pouch of important nutrients, will feed her while she is still growing and developing inside the egg.

days 2–45

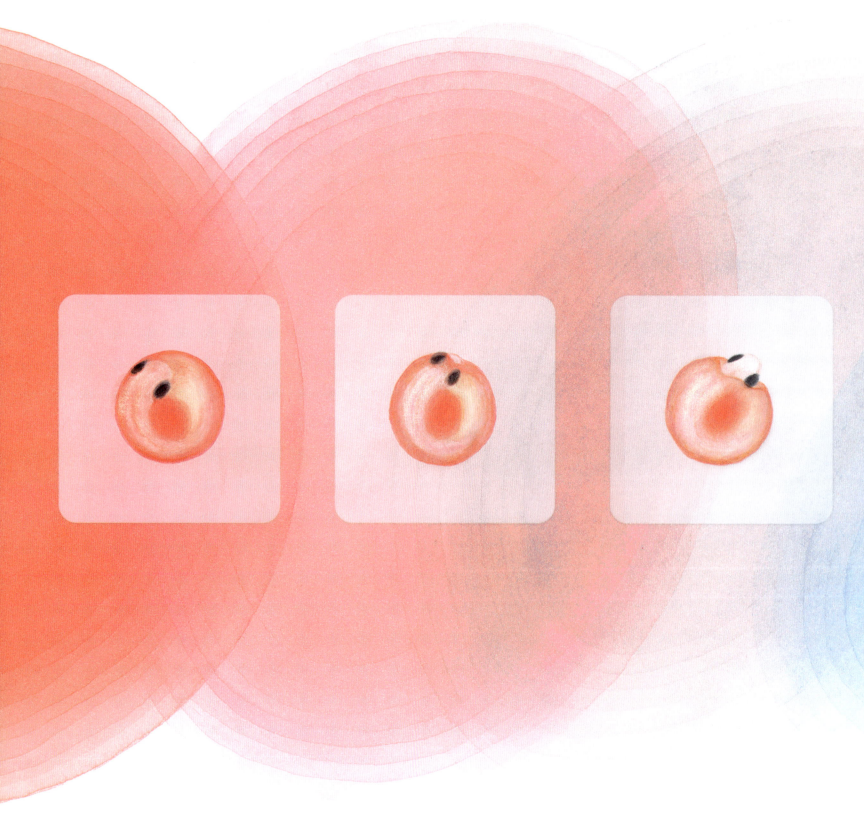

For a while, she has enough oxygen in the embryo, but as she grows, she will need more to survive. After about a month, she breaks free of the outer membrane of the egg and enters the oxygen-rich water.

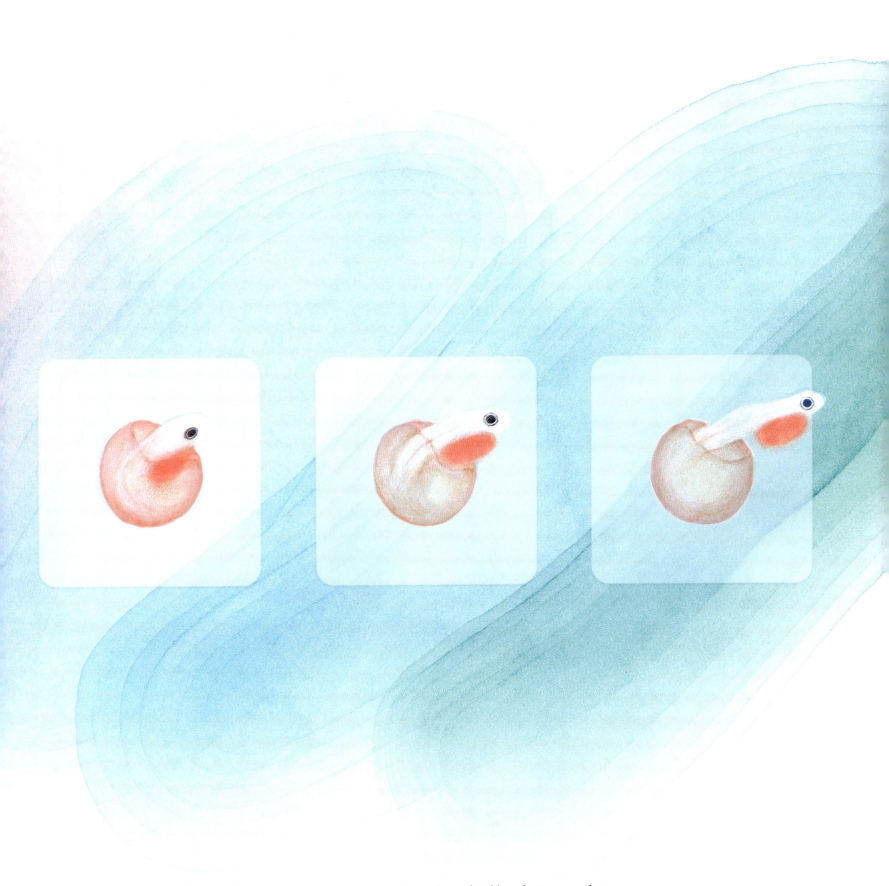

The yolk sac stays attached to her belly during this new phase of life, continuing to feed her before she can find her own food. She is now an alevin!

days 45–60

Small and vulnerable, she hides in the nooks and crannies of the river gravel. During the day, her orange belly makes her extra visible to predators . . .

so she tends to be more active at night. Under the cover of darkness, she shyly ventures out of the gravel to explore the open waters of the river.

days 45–60

In around two weeks, once she has fully absorbed the yolk . . .

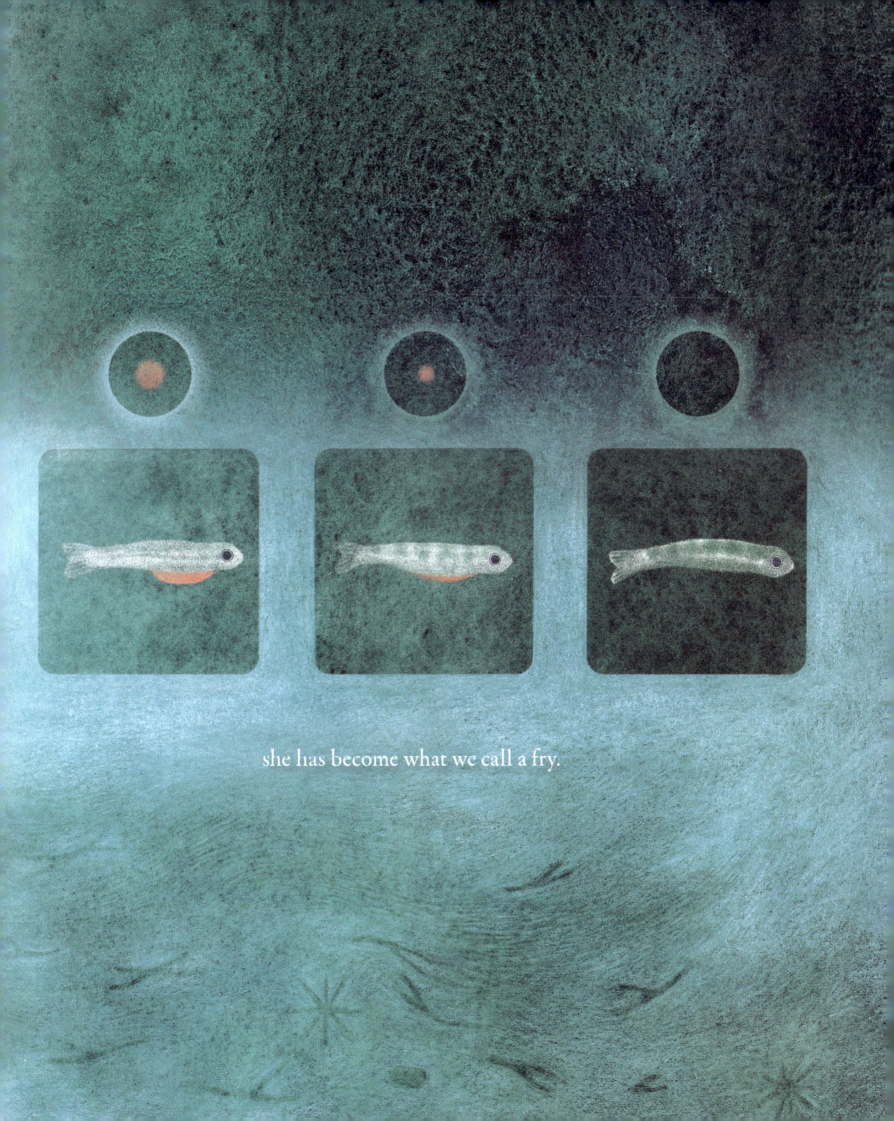
she has become what we call a fry.

days 60–560

The Pacific salmon is bigger now, but she is still small and vulnerable to predators like birds, otters, and larger fish!

To avoid them, she becomes adept at hiding in dark pools and protected spots. Her patterned markings help her camouflage especially well against the rocks and pebbles in the water.

days 60–560

As days pass and seasons change, she grows bigger and stronger. On a bright spring day, after more than a year in the river, she feels a deep instinct to travel west.

It is time to begin her great journey to the ocean!

days 560–650

Guided by the call of the salt and the sea, she swims downstream toward the mouth of the river, where it enters a large estuary called Puget Sound.

She will stay in the estuary for about three weeks, as her body undergoes a very special transformation called smolting.

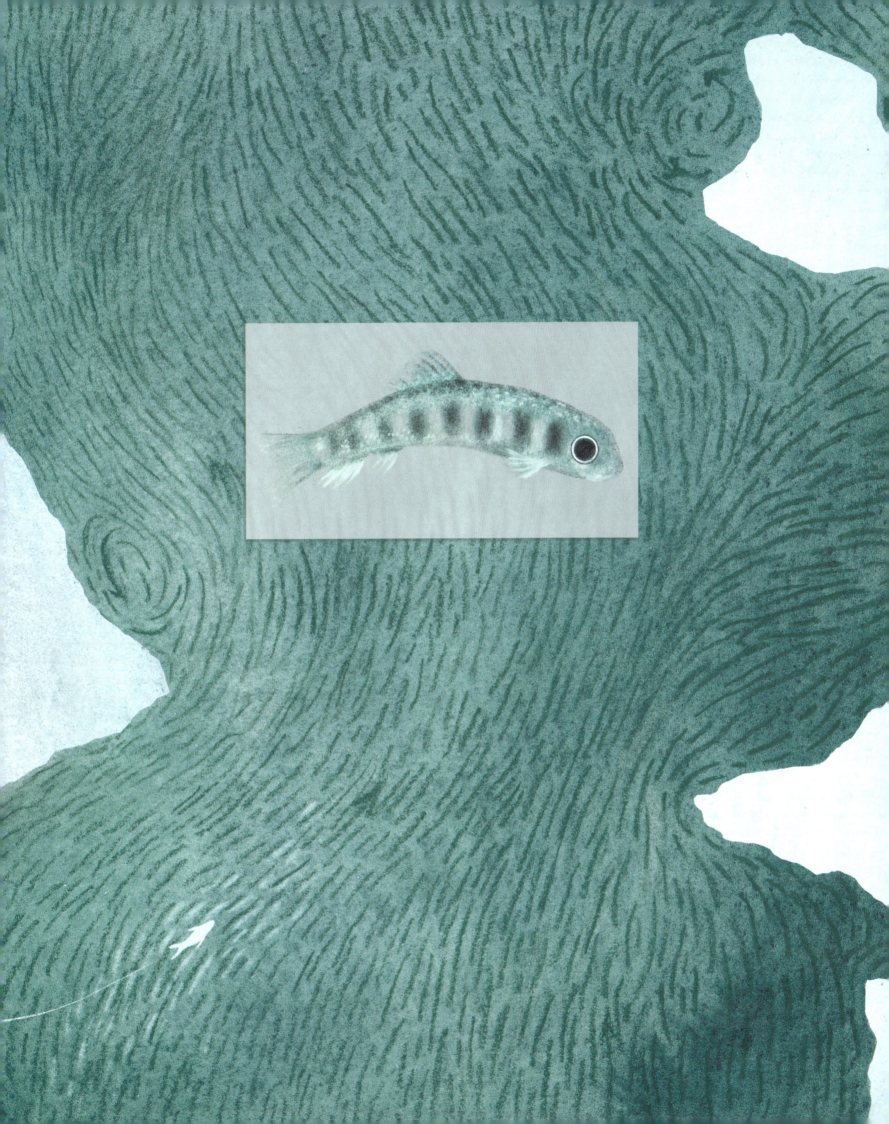

days 560–650

During the process of smolting, her body adapts to prepare her for the saltwater environment of the ocean, and the dark markings and green sheen on her body take on a silvery sparkle.

This silvery coating over her scales will help her blend into the lighter surface waters of the open ocean and hide from new, more dangerous predators like seals, sharks, and even orcas!

From Puget Sound, she will swim and swim until . . .

days 650–1,380

...finally, she reaches the Pacific Ocean!

She will spend most of her adult life here, surrounded by a vast expanse of deep, blue saltwater. There is so much to explore! Her new home is full of strange new creatures, like coral and jellyfish and sea turtles.

days 650–1,380

In this phase of adulthood, she will travel hundreds and even thousands of miles across the northern areas of the Pacific Ocean.

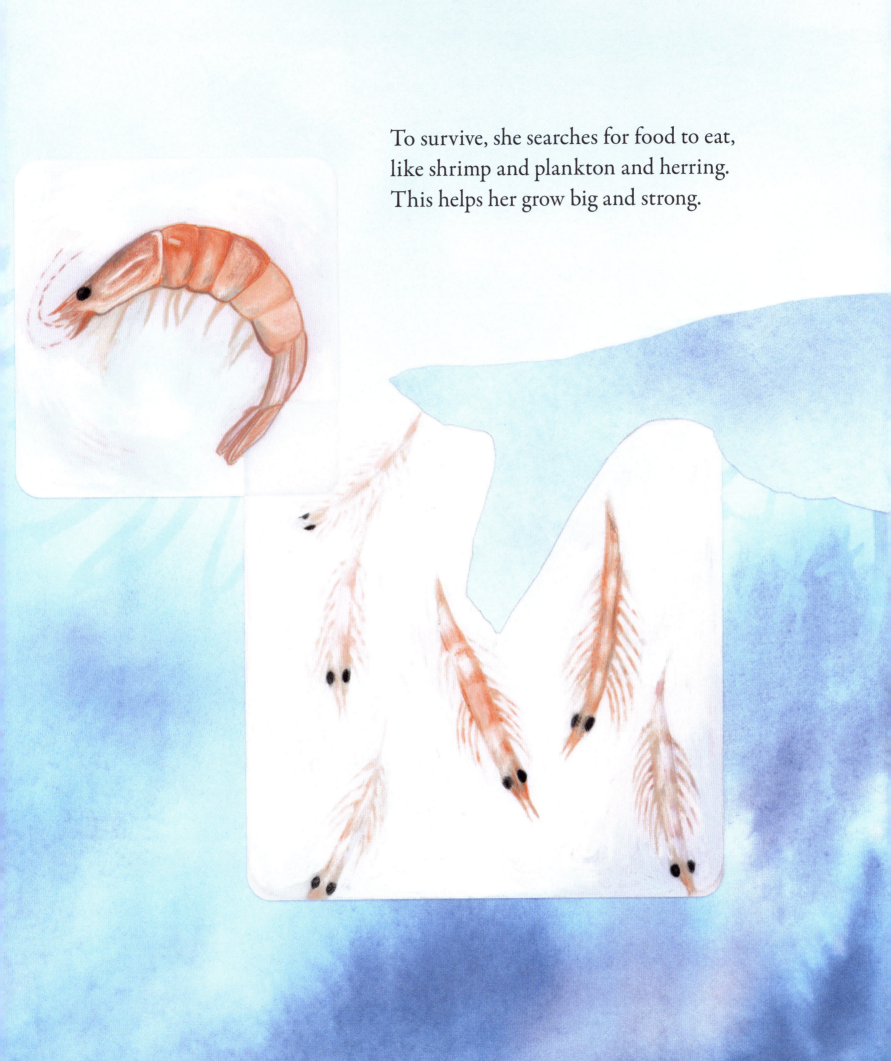

To survive, she searches for food to eat, like shrimp and plankton and herring. This helps her grow big and strong.

days 1,380–1,450

After around two years in the ocean, she will feel a deep instinct to return to the place where she was born. Her journey will be arduous and challenging—and she will be very lucky to complete it.

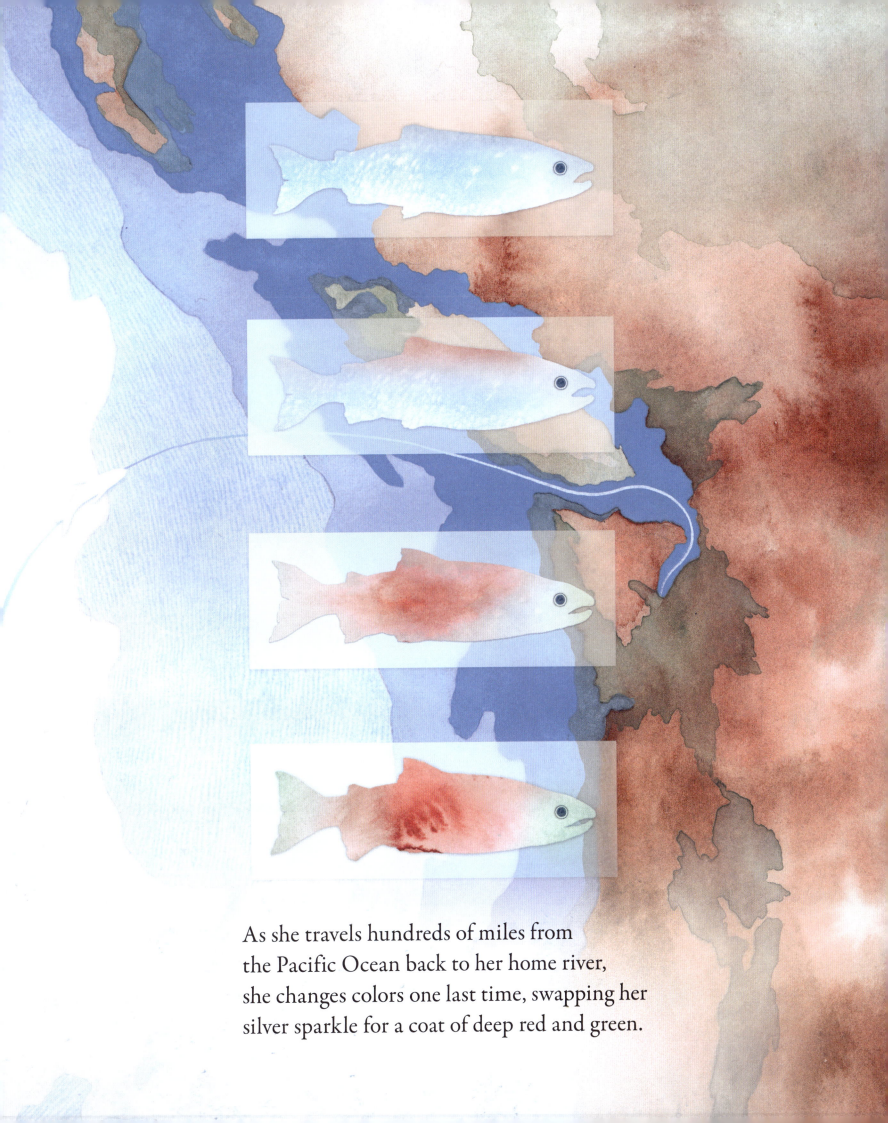

As she travels hundreds of miles from the Pacific Ocean back to her home river, she changes colors one last time, swapping her silver sparkle for a coat of deep red and green.

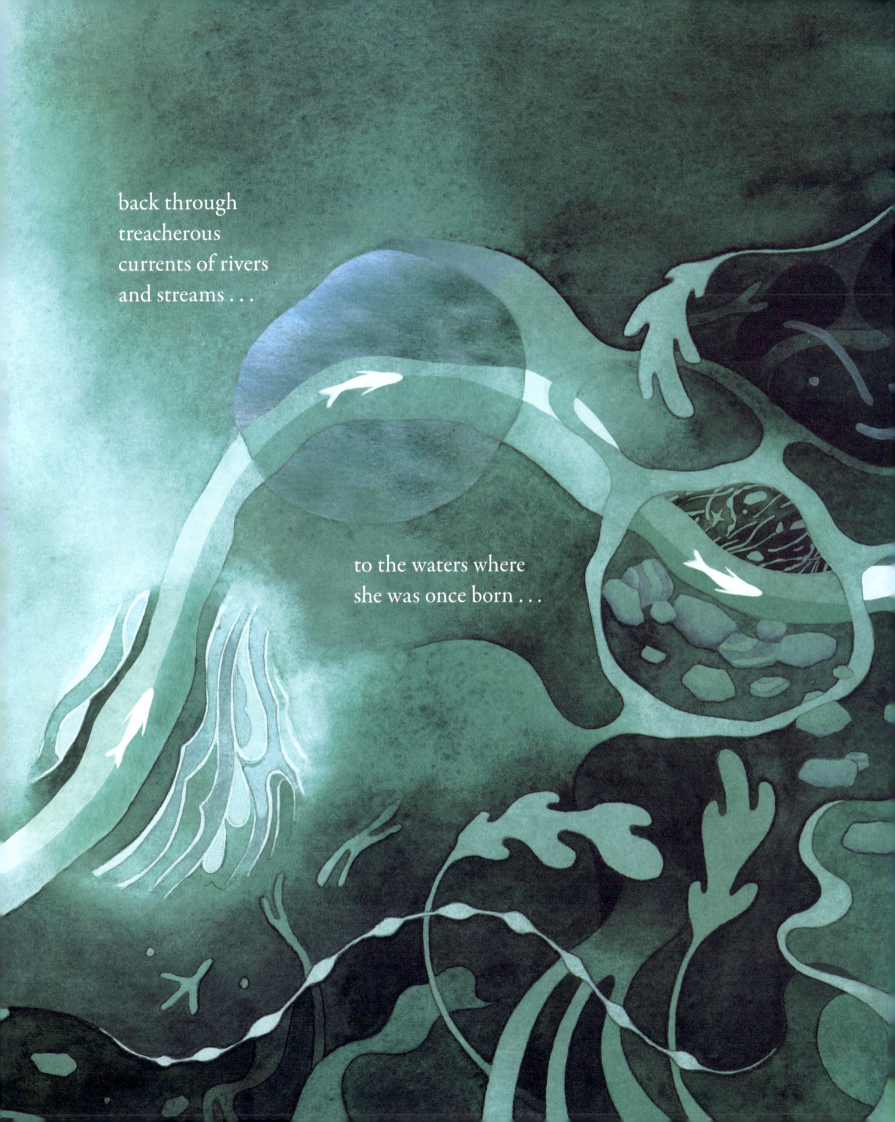

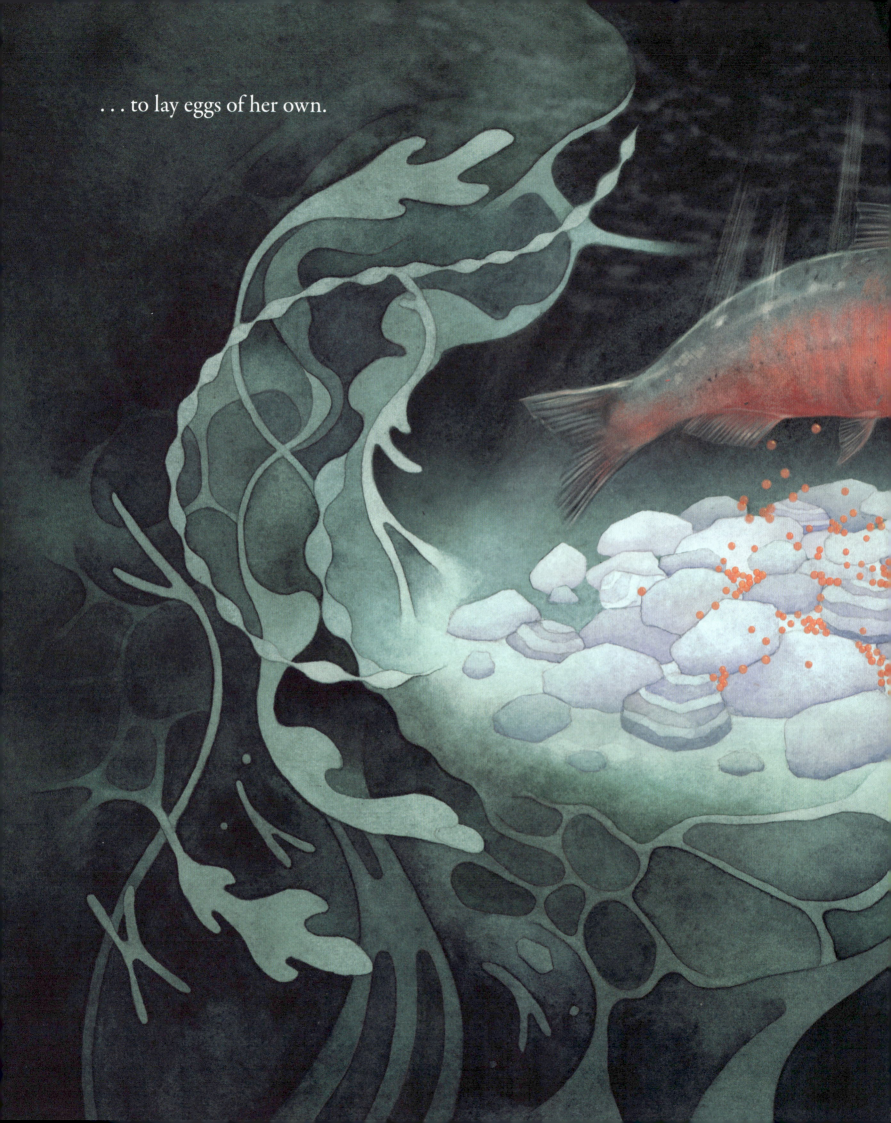
. . . to lay eggs of her own.

A NOTE FROM THE AUTHOR

Growing up in North Georgia, I spent countless hours outdoors—making mud pies, building forts out of leaves and branches, and splashing in the small creek behind our house. My sister and I would comb the banks for treasures, sifting through the silt and sand for sparkly stones and tiny clams. Those days were filled with endless exploration and imagination, where every forest, field, and stream promised a new adventure.

In fourth grade, our class learned about the ocean and the incredible creatures that call it home. The same sense of awe I'd felt in the woods returned as I learned more about the flora and fauna that live in our oceans, rivers, and lakes. This love for life—both big and small—along with my passion for telling stories through art, led me to study biology and design in college.

As someone who has always loved fish (especially salmon!), it has been a true joy to tell the remarkable story of their life cycle and the incredible journey they make between the ocean and their spawning rivers. The salmon run is a testament to the amazing determination of salmon to return home, despite the dangerous predators, harsh currents, and thousands of miles of open water they face along the way.

The specific coho salmon in this book begins her journey as a tiny egg in the Duwamish River. This location was based on my research on coho salmon, where I was able to find scientific records of their spawning locations in Washington. Drawing from these records and documented paths of salmon migrations, I mapped an approximate path for her journey from the Duwamish River to the Pacific Ocean, which measures a distance of more than 800 miles!

In the summer of 2023, I had the privilege of witnessing the Pacific salmon run firsthand. Crouched by the river, I watched in awe as groups of salmon swam past me—streaks of red and deep green slicing through the water, scales shimmering in the afternoon sun. Seeing so many salmon moving together was a truly magical and unforgettable experience.

Seeing the salmon run reminded me of something I've known since I was a kid— magic isn't limited to the world of fairy tales or fictional adventures you might find in books, cartoons, and movies. There is magic and wonder hidden in the natural world, all around us. From the tiniest plankton to the tallest tree, every living thing has its own special story to tell—just waiting for someone to take notice.

I hope *Salmon Run* inspires you to keep your eyes and ears open and your mind curious. Most of all, I hope this story takes you into your backyard, your neighborhood creek, or your local park—to find some magic of your own!

–*Annie*

THE LIFE CYCLE

- **EGG:** Salmon eggs are small, ranging from ¼ inch to ½ inch in size (depending on species of salmon), and are translucent with a reddish hue. A female coho salmon can lay anywhere between two thousand and six thousand eggs!

- **ALEVIN:** Alevins are about an inch long and have orange-colored yolk sacs attached to their bellies. They are fragile and tend to remain hidden in gravel, avoiding light and predators as they develop.

- **FRY:** Fry are around 1 to 2 inches long, with a silver body and small fins. They develop dark markings (called parr marks) on their sides, which help them blend in with their surroundings as they feed on plankton, insects, and small organic matter.

- **SMOLT:** Smolts develop a silver coloration that helps them camouflage in the ocean. They undergo smoltification, a process that allows them to adapt to saltwater, becoming sleek and streamlined for their ocean journey.

- **JUVENILE ADULT:** By this stage, salmon will have grown to be around 24 to 30 inches long and are silver in color. Young adult salmon spend their days foraging for food in the ocean and will travel long distances—up to 34 miles per day.

- **SPAWNING ADULT:** Adult salmon undergo dramatic physical changes: Their bodies shift from silver to vibrant reds, oranges, or greens, depending on the species. Males may develop a hooked snout and a humped back, while females maintain a more streamlined shape as they travel back to spawn in their home river.

COHO SALMON

The salmon featured in this book is a coho salmon, one of the six species of Pacific salmon that live in the waters of the Pacific Northwest. In the United States, they can be found in Washington, Oregon, Northern California, parts of Northern Alaska, as well as coastal regions on the west coast of Canada. Coho salmon are commonly called silver salmon because of their silvery appearance in the ocean. Known by the scientific name *Oncorhynchus kisutch*, adult cohos can be identified by their dark metallic blue or greenish backs with silver sides and a light belly, and usually have a lifespan of three to four years. On average, they weigh around 8 to 12 pounds (about the weight of a small dog) and can grow up to 30 inches long!

GET MORE INFORMATION INCLUDING A GLOSSARY OF TERMS AND FREE DOWNLOADS:

www.redcometpress.com/salmonbackmatter